Getting Inspired

Get Clear about What You Love to Do and Do Well

Eric Asbeck

Getting Inspired

Printed by:
CreateSpace Independent Publishing Platform

Copyright © 2017, What Business To Start, LLC

Published in the United States of America

ISBN-13: 978-1974362974
ISBN-10: 1974362973

For more information on 90-Minute Books including finding out how you can publish your own lead generating book, visit www.90minutebooks.com or call (863) 318-0464

Here's What's Inside…

Introduction

I'm Eric Asbeck, also known as "Your Next Move Business Coach." I'm going to talk about five simple steps you can take to find a business idea you love. What I'm going to share with you is one piece of work that we do when helping people get inspired about their business again. It's part of the first step in my system to create a business around your passions and your life, rather than your business taking over everything. This has opened up a lot of new possibilities for me and for a number of the people I've worked with more closely. I hope it does for you too!

My promise to you is to show you how to get clear about what you love to do and do well. Along the way, we'll talk about the source of powerful motivation for you to enthusiastically do what it takes to be successful. You'll find a surprisingly simple way to get into inspired action. You'll see how to communicate clearly about what you want to do next. And after we've done all that, we'll talk about how to get really clear about a business that's right for you – but you'll only hear about it after I have thoroughly delivered on my promise.

Getting clear is so important. When I worked with Maria, she was at a crossroads, trying to pursue several directions with her business. They were all really important to her, and she couldn't see a way to balance them all. We had a discovery session to get at what was really going on, then, after we worked more closely together, she said, "Eric has the uncanny ability to set the stage for clarity and focus. His thoughtful questions and guidance helped me to identify the obstacles that have prevented me from making my next best move." I was so happy to see her freed up and clear about where she wanted to go.

As I said, what I'm going to teach you today is one powerful move to get clear about what you love to do and do well. You'll have this available to you anytime you're feeling off course and want to re-tune your direction. It's part of the first step in my system to help you find a business right for you. That's our agenda.

Let me tell you a little bit about how I came to be doing this work. Back in high school, I was good in math and physics. I was also a gymnast and a competitive swimmer. I played first-chair clarinet in the band, and saxophone in a rock group called the Freedom Express. I really had fun with that group. We played a number of gigs in and around Charleston, West Virginia, where I grew up.

I ended up coming down with mononucleosis and was really dragging. With that, and because everybody wanted a little more money, they ended up kicking me out. This really broke my heart. I had some very good friends in the group, and I had thought they would watch my back. That didn't happen.

It really put me on a path. I realized that I would have to chart my own course and take care of things for myself, find my own North Star. Looking back, I realize getting kicked out of the group and finding my own way was the start of a guiding theme in the work that I do now.

I got my undergraduate degree in Industrial Engineering and Operations Research. It involves ways to make people and processes more effective and how to make better decisions. Had I been left to my own devices, I wouldn't have gone into engineering. My dad urged me to do that with the promise, "Get your engineering degree, and then you can do whatever you want."

I graduated and became an Industrial Engineer with Reynolds Metals. I was in their Corporate Industrial Engineering Group. We would travel to different locations around the U.S. and conduct industrial engineering studies in their foundries and plants.

After about a year of that, they said, "Congratulations, you've done really well! You get to have your very own foundry. Do that work for 10 years or so, and then maybe you can come back and do work in our industrial engineering group again." This was not what I wanted.

I went through some pretty dark times during that period. I was ready to give up. I thought maybe I couldn't really do what my dad promised and have work I really loved, so I began investing in myself.

A New Path

I made my first bold move and returned to school. I considered medicine and realized it wasn't a good fit. I made a pivot and received my MS in Systems Engineering from Case Western Reserve University and joined Bell Labs as a Systems Engineer, where I was involved in the creation of a number of highly successful new products and services for AT&T®.

In the evenings, I got my MBA with a focus on new venture development. I really loved the business side, and I wanted to make a move from Bell Labs to AT&T, but it wasn't so easy to do that. I tried a bunch of different things. What I finally found that worked was my S.A.L.S.A. Scan™, which is the powerful tool that I'm going to teach you today. I used it to get clear about what I loved to do and do well. That clarity let me continue investing in myself by taking on special projects, and I established a track record of successes focused on the work I loved.

Having that focus is so important. When I worked with Denyne, she wanted to expand her holistic interior design business online. As a baseline, we assessed her current situation, her starting point. We created some real-world next steps to get her started building the systems she needed, plus some online tools to support her virtual services. Through a lot of focused work, she's since expanded her service area to all of New England, plus virtual services worldwide.

She said, "Eric is a master at helping you define your focus and getting you started on a clear path to productivity and success in your business. His advice is simple, easy to follow, and just makes sense! He's very easy to talk to and a great listener - which is so important in a business coach. I've had many mentors over the years, and Eric is definitely a shining star." I was so glad to have the opportunity to help her along her path.

With my track record of successes, I was able to take another leap. I became a product manager at AT&T in a hot internal startup. It was a really exciting time. I created a new offer that won over $25M in business with AT&T's most demanding customers and grew the business 10%. I took a chance and made the change. I loved it, and I excelled.

I moved to NCR and became the Global Program Director for NCR's quarter-billion-dollar Cisco® program. We had business in about 63 countries around the world. I got to establish close personal relationships with people all over the world, from Japan to Australia and a number of places in Europe and the Middle East. I also got to know some Latin American and South American folks. It was quite an amazing job.

From there, I moved to Cisco Systems®. I was a business development manager in their strategic alliances organization. I helped develop joint services and put together some joint deals between Cisco and some of their biggest partners, like IBM, HP®, and consultancies like Accenture, BearingPoint, and Capgemini.

Throughout that time, I created new offers and services that won over $125 million in new business. What a fun ride!

Along the way over the past 15 years, I've also devoted some of my time coaching individuals and groups to create a life they love, with outstanding results.

Now I have my own business helping people get clear, focused, and back in action, producing purposeful results and loving what they do.

My Biggest Inspiration

As I was preparing this for you, I took a moment to step back and reflect. What was it that really drew me to be an "intrepreneur" creating new businesses within the companies where I worked and then to be an outright entrepreneur?

The answer really comes down to my dad. He was born in Germany and came to the United States at age nine on an actual boat. He grew up in Cleveland, got his undergraduate and Master's degrees in Chemical Engineering, and ended up getting a scholarship to the University of Berlin to do his PhD. He arrived in Berlin just before Hitler invaded Poland. For several years, he was fine. America wasn't part of the war, and it was actually a privileged status to be an American citizen student.

Then, of course, Japan invaded Pearl Harbor, and the U.S. declared war on both Japan and Germany. At that point he was on the other side. He ended up being interned in the city of Berlin. Fortunately, he wasn't in a concentration camp, but he wasn't allowed to leave Berlin; he was stuck there during the war. I just recently finished publishing a book that he'd written about that - some exciting times.

He ended up as a chemical researcher with Union Carbide in Charleston, West Virginia, where I grew up. He was quite successful, but he still had that immigrant dream of starting his own business. While I was growing up, he pursued his dream on the side; he invented, designed, patented, and built a prototype for a 28-foot amphibious motorhome. It was designed for a person to drive it into the water, pull up the wheels, and use it as a boat.

My dad was prepared to start manufacturing his invention and launch a business selling them. He had the loans lined up and the lease space. He was ready to sign everything when the first oil crisis of the 1970s hit. My dad's invention was a real gas hog, and it used petroleum products in the fiberglass hull too. He took a look at the situation and thought, "I've got a young family, and I just can't risk it," and so he backed off.

A couple of years went by, things got better, and he did another round of lining everything up. He was, again, within a few months of getting ready to sign on the dotted line, and the second, even worse gas crisis hit. That's the one everybody remembers, with the gas lines. My dad backed off from his dream again.

As it turns out, he never started that business. He ended up receiving an offer to go into business with my uncle in Cleveland. He moved the family there. It was a lower-risk offer. The opportunity wasn't quite as big, but my dad did okay.

He's still with us today, and even now he speaks somewhat whimsically about what might have been. My dad never realized his dream, and so I ask myself, "What about me?" and "What about you?"

Surprises

There's another thing I want to tell you. I have a kind of cancer called multiple myeloma, which is a cancer of the blood. It causes bone fractures and those sorts of things. My career was going along really well, I was very happy with what was going on, and, suddenly, I found myself unable to walk. I was literally crawling around, misdiagnosed with fractured ribs, and finally was told I had a tumor in my spine. I was on bedrest for a number of months and on disability. I underwent back surgery and a stem-cell transplant. Multiple myeloma is treatable, not curable, but it's being well managed. It's been over a decade now, and I'm doing great. My game-plan is to keep doing great until a cure is found.

That was a really scary time when I found myself literally on my back and stuck like that. The first thing I did was to look at businesses and franchises that I could possibly be involved with from my home. That's when I realized how much I wanted to create a business of my own.

As it turns out, I came off disability and continued to work for Cisco. It was a great company and a great job. And yet it was similar to my dad's trade-off, and it just made better sense to stick with my job. During that period of time, I also got myself really grounded, really present. I thought, "This is what's happening; this is where I stand," and I asked myself, "What can I create from here?"

Also during that time, a friend of mine called who I had helped quite a bit over the course of a few years and was a two-time breast cancer survivor. She called me from her home in Dallas and said, "Listen, Eric, you're going to survive this. What's your life going to be about after you get through this?" It didn't take me but a second. It was right on the tip of my tongue to say, "I'm passionate about seeing other people live their passions. It really lights me up." I love it when people are really doing the things they're passionate about.

I also want to tell you a little bit about my friend Jeff, because Jeff is the reason I decided to take the leap and go into my own business. Jeff and I were really good buddies. We would get together once a week, grab some dinner, and do various things. Besides the usual hanging out and shooting the breeze, we actually talked about some pretty significant stuff and supported each other. It was one of those rare, lucky relationships that guys sometimes have; he was a really good friend. As it turns out, he ended up coming down with a disease of his own that was similar to what I have, and he wasn't doing too well. He tried a bunch of things, including homeopathic remedies and similar treatments.

One night, Jeff and I were getting ready to go out to dinner when he said, "Look, I'd like to go to a really nice place." We sat there across the table from each other, enjoying a fine meal, and he paused, looked me right in the eye, and said, "Listen, buddy, I want you to go for your dreams. Will you do that?" Of course, I said yes, and we moved on to the rest of our dinner.

The next night he was out on a date, and he had a heart attack and died. What a shock! I guess you never know how long you've got or what may be around the next corner. I really missed his friendship, and something hit me really deeply. You can imagine that deep down in the ocean of myself, things started to shift and move. I thought, "Some of Jeff's last words to me were, 'Will you go for your dreams?'" I thought, "If not now, when?" That was the thing that got me started along this path, focusing my attention on building a business that I love.

This book is for you if you're not sure what you want to do – if you knew, you could come up with a plan. Maybe you've been compromising, doing things you do well and what other people want, but it's not the authentic you. Or maybe you're fed up with this buyer's job market, commute, and job options that take over your life, and you have entrepreneurship in your blood. Perhaps you wake up every morning dreading the business you've created. Or you just feel lost and haven't dared confess it. You're in the right place if you are willing to invest in yourself and do what it takes.

With this book, you'll learn the source of powerful motivation to enthusiastically do what it takes to be successful. I'll show you how to get clear about what you love to do AND do well. We'll talk about ways to use this to create a business or work you love. Finally, I'll show you how to get clear about your next move in creating a business around your passions and your life.

I hope this book inspires you to get clear about what you love to do and do well. I hope it encourages you to go for your dreams and build a business and life that you love.

To Your Success!

Eric Asbeck

Getting Inspired!

Now let's shift gears and talk about the source of powerful motivation to enthusiastically do what it takes to be successful. And before you're done reading this, I promise I'll show you how you can take it further. In fact, you might want to get yourself in front of a computer because I have something special for you, and I'll give you the page where you can see it.

Here's an exercise I'd like you to do: Draw a 2x2 matrix; a table with two columns and two rows. Across the top, label the columns "Can" and "Can't." Along the side, label the rows "Love" and "Hate."

Now put some labels in these boxes, starting with the Hate-Can't box. I call that one "Unlikely" because it's really unlikely that you'll find yourself doing work that you hate and that you can't do very well or can't do at all, and if you do find yourself there, you're not going to be there for very long!

You really want to be in the Love-Can quadrant. I call that "Bliss" because if you're doing work that you love and that you do really well, it can't get much better than that.

You could find yourself in one of those other two quadrants. You could find yourself in the Love-Can't quadrant; I call that "Development." Maybe there are things that you know that you like doing, but perhaps you don't have the right credentials or the work experience to give you an entrée into doing that thing you love. That's an opportunity for personal and professional development: training, programs, and volunteering. We'll talk more about that in a moment.

The other place you could find yourself is in the Hate-Can quadrant. I label that, "What to do?" "Hate" doesn't necessarily mean that you loathe it. It could be that you would just rather not be there; you would rather be doing something else. In my case, I didn't hate the technical work I was doing at Bell Labs, but I knew that I really wanted to do the business side of things much more.

What do you do in this situation? Some people think they just need to press harder, and they end up feeling more miserable. One thing you can do instead is come up with a plan to transition. I'll talk more about that as well.

Let's say you find yourself in that Hate-Can quadrant, and you get promoted to managing a bunch of people who are doing that work. That doesn't sound great, does it?

I was taking a class some years ago, and the leader was working with someone who said she really hated her job. The leader suggested that she take on loving her work, loving her job. It was a mindset shift, really; she should just give it a try, play with it.

What would it be like if instead of constantly thinking, "I hate this, I hate it," you really took on loving it? The woman in my class was very coachable and willing to give it a try. Over the course of the rest of the program, as she changed her mindset, things did shift for her. Even though her situation wasn't perfect for her, things got a lot better.

That point really got driven home for me a few years ago when I was coaching Aaron, who was looking at finding another job. As part of the coaching that I did with him, I helped him come up with ideas for how to find another position. As an aside, I tossed out this idea: "If it doesn't work out, you could take on loving the job you're in."

As it turns out, over the course of time, his opportunities for a different job fell through. About six months after I had worked with him, he actually made a point of calling me up and thanking me for the suggestion I made about taking on loving his current job. He had looked at where he stood and taken the action available to him right there, my off-hand suggestion. He ended up getting a small raise, then a small promotion. That led to a job at another company. He told me that shifting his mindset made a huge difference for him. Mindset does matter.

Leveraging the Sweet Spot between What You Love to Do and What You Do Well

Let me tell you how I used this in my own career transition. I used the process I'm going to teach you today to get clear about what I love to do and do well, bolster what was in my Love-Can't category, take on some special projects, and shift from the Hate-Can to the Love-Can quadrant. Looking back, I realize it all goes back to that moment in my childhood rock group, Freedom Express, when I realized that I needed to chart my own course. This process really helped me to do that.

When I first started working with Barbara, who was an actor and an artist, I didn't realize that she was also an entrepreneur. When she was in college, her dad owned a company called Computer World, which was kind of like Best Buy and Circuit City. Computer World is gone now, but there was a period of time where they had over 800 locations around the world. Barbara rose up in that company and was actually the CEO for a while; however, she much preferred acting and artistic pursuits.

In our discovery session, she got really clear that she wanted a way to pursue her acting and artistic passions and still contribute to the family finances. When I worked more closely with her, we went through the S.A.L.S.A. Scan™. As a result, Barbara got in touch with something that had been in the back of her mind that she'd never put a voice to. She wrote out a whole vision for herself of things that she had never articulated as clearly as this. From there, we looked at how she could achieve that vision and some real-world steps that she could take in the present; the first, second, third, and fourth steps in my system.

Barbara sent a note to me, saying, "It was the favorite thing I've done lately. I loved it! I haven't felt as tuned in to what is really me in a while. I feel so much more inspired by my vision since I've renewed it for myself. I feel excited to start moving in that direction." Seeing her so lit up and focused is so rewarding for me.

The question is: What do you love to do, and what do you do well? I call those your sweet spots: things that you both love to do and that you do well. How do you get clear about what you love to do and do well? Get ready to take notes. As I said, this is one piece in the first step of my B.L.I.S.S. Builder™ System to create a business around the passions in your life, rather than fitting your life in around your work or your business. I used this to make the shift from the technical to the business side of my work. You can do it too.

I call this process the S.A.L.S.A. Scan™. I call it that because I do ballroom and Latin dancing socially, and I realized that I could come up with the acronym S.A.L.S.A., just to have some fun with it. There's structure behind this process. I have structures like this to help you systematically work through all the steps, so you can get results. And before we're finished, I'll show you how to get more. I'll actually show you my B.L.I.S.S. Builder™ System. I'll show you what it takes. And for those who want to take it further, I'll show you how. I'd be honored to be your mentor to find a business idea that is right for you.

Like I said, this little tool has really opened up new possibilities for people I've worked with. I'll give you a quick overview of the steps, and then we'll dive into them one-by-one. In the acronym S.A.L.S.A., "S" is for "Set-Up", "A" is for "Add", "L" is for "Love", the second "S" is for "Skills", and the final "A" is for "Aim". Altogether, S.A.L.S.A. is: Set-Up, Add, Love, Skills, and Aim.

"Set-Up" is when you set up your worksheet. Your worksheet is the thing that's going to provide the structure for you to do the work and to do it in a systematic way so that you can keep track of things. It's really important to have a structure like this, because it makes the work go a whole lot more smoothly.

This worksheet is a three-column table. Of the three columns, the first one is "Time Period". The next column I call "Experiences, Activities, and Training". The third column I call "Notes". Once you've got those three columns set up, you're going to set up the rows, which are the different time periods in your life. The first row that I have for myself I called "Pre-High School", because there were a few things that happened when I was younger and through that period of time that I wanted to include in my experiences, activities, and training. The next row I called "High School". Then I have a row for "Sports or Other Extracurricular Activities". Next, I have a row for "College" for my undergraduate degree. I also have additional, separate rows for my Master's in System Engineering and my MBA in New Venture Development. I also have a row for "Summer Jobs" that I had.

Next, I have rows for first job, second job, third job, and so forth. For example, I was with Bell Labs and AT&T for about nine years, and over the course of that time, I occupied a number of different job roles. To account for these, I made a separate row for each of those roles within that time, rather than trying to put everything in one big lump, because I had some different experiences there. I ended up with rows for Bell Labs, rows for AT&T, more rows for NCR, and so forth.

Finally, I have three extra rows that I use to capture things that are kind of outside of the norm. I have one that I call "Volunteering", and I have a couple of different things that fall into that. As a catchall, I have a row for "Hobbies", and then I have a final catchall at the end that I call "Other Outside

Interests". To review, those last three are Volunteering, Hobbies, and Other Outside Interests.

Step Two is "Add" and involves adding your experiences. You want to lay out all the different experiences, activities, and training you've had that would fall under each of your time periods. Certainly, you want to include all of your official, professional job experience.

In addition to working at Bell Labs and AT&T, I had summer jobs. For example, I was a short order chef one summer. During another part of my undergraduate experience, I was a co-op student, going to school for a quarter and then working someplace related to my field, industrial engineering operations and research. I gained professional experience that way, and it also paid my way through school.

You also want to make sure to include any volunteering that you've done. For example, when I was doing my pre-med work, I volunteered at a hospital, in particular in the Emergency Room. That was a pretty memorable experience, so there are some things I included on my worksheet that were related to that time.

Another thing in terms of volunteering, I told you I had multiple myeloma. I am on the steering committee for the multiple myeloma support group in my area here so that we make sure that we have some continuity with that program because it really does some good work for folks.

Let's see. What more do I tell you? When you think about the other training that you've done, it's not just your formal college degrees that count here.

You want to include other training as well. For instance, I have a number of certificates that I earned, and I took a whole series of courses at AT&T on building your business, counselor sales person, things like that. Those things are a part of my experience. I mentioned previously that I did a variety of sports, especially when I was in high school, so under Hobbies I listed gymnastics, swimming, and also the clarinet, saxophone, and rock group. I included my ballroom and Latin social dancing hobby as well.

You want to take time to really review your experiences when filling out your worksheet. For instance, when I was in high school, I got a life-saving certificate. My idea at the time, before I knew that I would be doing the co-op work in college, was to be a lifeguard at the pool as my summer job. It turns out that I didn't use my life-saving certificate for that, but on two separate occasions, I saved somebody from drowning, and it was all due to the training I received. That goes to show that you never know where your experience will come into play. You want to capture all of that in your worksheet.

You also want to take the time to really engage your family and friends, people who know and love you, and have them help you as you fill this out and as you go through the subsequent steps. Here's an example: When I was talking to my sister Carol about these things, she said, "You know, Eric, one thing about you is that you're really good at going out and finding these Internet tools that could be pretty helpful and then really explaining to people how they can apply them." I knew I did that, but it didn't really occur to me until I was speaking with her that doing that was something I should list on my worksheet. It turns out to be something I love to do and do well. And I'm using that now in my business, both for myself and for my clients.

The idea is to engage those folks who know you and get their help as you fill this out. You want to add your experiences very thoroughly because the next steps go pretty quickly, and the better you do this step, the more value you're going to get out of the next ones.

Now the fun begins. Step Three is "Love", what you love to do. I want you to go through all those experiences and highlight all the ones that you love to do. Be generous with yourself. I don't want you to edit this by saying, "Oh, well, I can't see how that could possibly relate to work that I'm going to do, a business that I'm going to have, a job that I might want to take in the future." Don't edit yourself. If you love it, highlight it. You can even check in with the people who love you to see if there is anything you missed. See what I mean about this part going pretty quickly? I'll say again, take the time to thoroughly list your experiences first, before jumping to this and the next steps!

Step Number Four is "Skills", what you do well. Underline everything that you do well. Again, this is a case where you really want to listen to other people's thoughts and be generous with yourself. You may be inclined to be a little humble or rough on yourself about something. You might also hear other people say something you're good at that you had never thought about. It might just be that you are your harshest critic and maybe a little bit reluctant to give yourself credit for something that you do well. Still, you hear other people say,

"You're crazy! You give great presentations!" or "You're really good in front of an audience," or whatever it might be. Simply underline all the things that you do well.

Step Five is the last step in the S.A.L.S.A. Scan™—"A" is for "Aim". You're going to look for patterns and what I call your "Sweet Spots". If you look at your worksheet, some entries are not marked, some are highlighted, some are underlined, and some are both highlighted and underlined. Guess what? Every single one of those things that are both highlighted and underlined is something you love to do and you do well. Pretty simple, right?

For my own worksheet, I collected all of those instances in a Microsoft Word document and then started to look for patterns, organizing them into similar groups. Create those groupings for yourself.

Once I'd gotten an idea of what things were commonly grouped together, I came up with descriptive names for each of those as functional skills. For example, when I used this worksheet for my field change, one of my functional skills was a knack for forming and leading teams. I did that well, and I liked to do it. Forming and leading teams to produce a particular result or achieve an outcome.

Sean had a series of businesses before we worked more closely together. When I knew him, he had built a business that was fairly successful. He appeared to be doing really well.

As time went on, I would check in with him. At first he would give me the long-answer version of how things were, but after a while I would ask, "How are you doing, Sean?" and he would respond, "Fine, buddy. How are you?" I couldn't get any more out of him.

All of a sudden, he just dropped out. He disappeared, and I wondered what happened. I tracked him down, and it turns out he had quit his business because he was miserable. His style is to keep pressing ahead and figure a way to make things work. He's so competent that most of the time he can, but not in this case, and the bottom fell out.

I said, "Well, what have you been up to?"

He replied, "I directed a high school musical. I've gotten some parts in shows in New York." It turns out he loves to do musical acting. He continued, "You know, maybe I'll just go get a job." I've known Sean for a while, and in the back of my mind, I was thinking, "You're a really talented entrepreneur, so that's like a no pass."

However, you can tell somebody something, and it has one kind of impact, but if they can show themselves, it has another level of impact. I had Sean do the S.A.L.S.A. Scan™, and I had him do another piece of work I called the B.L.I.S.S. Lifestyle Targeter™, where you take a look at all the different areas and relationships of your life and get really clear about what you want. My system provides the simple structures to guide you along.

Within about 36 hours of putting Sean on that track, he was running through the S.A.L.S.A. Scan™. He sent me a note that said, "Holy cow, Eric. I'm excited about getting into business again. And that's saying something because just a few weeks ago, I thought my days of being an entrepreneur were done."

Sean also got really clear when speaking with his wife about what he wanted in the different areas and relationships of his life. He had two non-negotiables: First, he wanted to continue to be able to actively pursue his acting career, and second, he wanted to have time with his wife on the weekends when he wasn't in rehearsals. If those weren't available with a business he was creating, it wasn't going to work.

Now he is building a business around his acting career and around those two non-negotiables. I had a chance to see him a little while back, and he had the lead role in the production of Kiss Me Kate by the Heights Players in Brooklyn, New York. That lead role is a pretty hefty role, and he knocked it out of the park.

I had a chance to meet Sean's wife and mother as well. When I met his wife and was talking to her, she got misty-eyed with tears of joy, and I realized the impact Sean's life change made on her. He went from being miserable to being able to pursue both his acting and a business that worked for him and his family. That was something I hadn't really seen until I had that experience with Sean. It's not just the people with whom I work who reap the benefits; the other people in their lives do too. I actually get goosebumps as I re-read this. That makes it all worthwhile.

How Getting Clear on What You Love to Do Leads to Work You Love

When I did my own field change, I took those functional skills that I'd learned about from the groupings of the things that I highlighted and underlined, and I put them into a functional résumé and then listed each of the experiences under the functional skill that lined up with each grouping. Even though employers don't necessarily like a functional résumé, it was really helpful for me to be able to see them grouped because it gave me a sense of what experiences I had that supported each of those functional skills. I got a sense of how current they were, whether they were new and recent or something from the past. It gave me the opportunity to ask, "How can I create some current experiences that highlight those functional skills that I know I love and do well?"

I worked with my management and did some special projects that let me do that. For example, I did some consultative technical sales support for a couple of AT&T's big customers, and I was part of a group that created business and technical plans for some new services that AT&T might provide. I ended up leading market research that included focus groups, visiting a number of customers, and describing what we were up to in order to test those ideas and see if they made sense.

I've worked with a number of people as part of a job-search team who have used volunteering in a couple of different ways. Ram, for example, was part of the pharmaceutical industry, and he got let go. He found an opportunity to do some volunteer business development work with a small company.

When he started out, he worked just a couple of hours, one day a week, but he did well and negotiated to expand that role and get a bit of pay for it.

Ram used that experience on his résumé and got himself a job that used his technical background and his new business-development skills. This job was something that wouldn't have been available to him if he hadn't done that volunteer work.

Allen recently landed a job. He did some volunteering, and he used it as a way of keeping his hand in the scientific work that he had been doing. He demonstrated his people skills and got a good reference from the person leading this particular volunteer group. Allen ended up landing a job that let him do the work he loved and get paid for it. He's a manager for an analytical lab now. Volunteering can be very powerful. The key point here is that this is an opportunity for you to invest in yourself and make something happen.

When you're clear about your sweet spots, what you love to do and do well, you can ASK for what you want, and you can also make better choices about opportunities that either become available to you or opportunities that you actively go out and seek that will move you in the direction you want to go.

When we work more closely together, we also use the work you do with your worksheet because it makes clear what you do well, and we can use it to talk about your areas of expertise. We can use it to develop business ideas that might make sense for you, and we can also identify areas where it might make sense for you to do some professional development.

The B.L.I.S.S. Builder™ System

Let's talk about ways to create a business that you love. Recall our 2x2 matrix of Can/Can't and Love/Hate. We need to get you into that Bliss quadrant of Love-Can. We also need to figure out what you may need to do in terms of personal and professional development to move some of the things for which you don't have the credentials and that you need into that quadrant. If you're finding yourself in the Hate-Can group, how can we shift things?

I help people who want to live life on their own terms and create a business around their passions and their life, rather than their business taking over everything, so let's work on giving you some clarity about your own North Star.

Have you thought lately, "I'm not sure what I want to do?" Maybe you ask yourself, "Why can't I figure this out?" It's so frustrating when you're not clear about where you're headed. Maybe you're even chastising yourself, thinking, "I should know." When you're not clear about where you're headed, you can end up taking a lot of action and dispersing your energy in too many directions, not actually getting anywhere.

I've heard people say that they feel that they're spinning around in circles or drowning in a soup. Some say they feel anxious every day, things like, "I dread giving more talks and having more conversations and making more sales because I'm building on something that's not really quite right for me or that I don't like. It's just not working." That's where people get stuck and distracted. After people work more closely with me, they say things like, "I feel like a weight has been lifted." If this sounds like you, you're someone I want to talk with.

Now that you have the results from the S.A.L.S.A. Scan™, you have a good start on some really great direction for a business idea. You understand exactly what goes into getting clear about what you love to do and do well. Now let me show you what it really takes to find a business you love, because what you love to do and do well is only one piece of the pie, right?

You have your Sweet Spots, but there's also what you want in your life and lifestyle, a bunch of possible business ideas, and how to choose your idea and move it forward. Now that you have your Sweet Spots and know how to use them, let me show you how to find a business idea that works for you and your life, the other pieces you're going to need that are going to actually make this whole thing work, OK?

So that's what I'm going to show you. And at the end, I'll show you how you can take this even deeper, if you want to work with me or talk to me more about it. Would you like to hear about the other pieces that will actually make a difference for you?

I have a five-step system called the B.L.I.S.S. Builder™ System where we dig way deeper.

When I worked more closely with Sharyn, she was a successful professional without job avenues that worked for her now. In our discovery session, we uncovered her entrepreneurial spirit and her best strategic next move. As we worked more closely together, we used my process and, well, let's hear it in her own words. "I was interested in starting my own company, but I was unsure of what I wanted to do and how to start out on my own. I connected with Eric and he walked me through his process with instructions and standard templates, adjusted for my needs. I now know where I want to go and what I want to do."

So what was the process we used? The first step in my B.L.I.S.S. Builder™ System is called "Baseline", where we get you grounded and open up new possibilities. The S.A.L.S.A. Scan™ is part of that first step, as are some other pieces. We also look at what you want for your life, lifestyle, and business. One of the biggest mistakes people make here is to try and jump ahead before they're clear about exactly where they stand right now.

The next step is Love, and that's where you really tune in and feel inspired by your vision. We'll start building what we call your "B.L.I.S.S. Yardstick™", which is a systematic way of saying, "What do YOU want?" and explicitly laying it out. There are some powerful ways we can use that B.L.I.S.S. Yardstick™.

The "I" in B.L.I.S.S. is for Inspiration. This is when you get clear about your North Star with a business idea that matches what you want and calls to your heart. We use your Yardstick to measure how your possible business ideas fit with what you want. We can even tweak and tune them so they fit even better. Then, after all the analysis, we step back and you chose a business idea that's right for you and calls to your heart.

Most people know they want to make a heart-centered choice, but they miss the part about being really clear about what they want and how all those business ideas line up with it. That's why it's in my system and I have worksheets and structures that make this simple.

The first "S" in B.L.I.S.S. is for Steps. We find a clear path to where you want to be and some real-world steps that you can take right now to move yourself forward.

The last "S" I call Support, and that includes ways to support your success and keep your vision alive. What kind of structures, systems, and tools can we put in place that would keep you organized to support you moving forward? Of course, when we work together more closely, I'm there to support you. It's so powerful when you know your North Star.

Deirdre had a successful and growing business teaching people how to speak and get results. We looked at some additional online tools to support her virtual services. We identified some additional venues for her programs. She's continued to grow her successful business locally and online. She said, "In a kind and direct manner, Eric gets to the heart of the matter. Eric does not let you continue to fool yourself with your excuses for why things can't happen. He's also great at suggesting next steps, especially where technology is involved. If you want to stay confused, don't work with Eric! If you want to take strategic forward movement, Eric is your man!" Love it!

I talked about the value of structure and how that can help you systematically do the work, and how we have structures for the work we do together. The other thing I want to point out, however, is that if you look back at my path, for example, you can see that it was not a straight line. Neither was Sean's. Or many other successful entrepreneurs.

Typically, people's paths are not straight. You can expect to cycle back. Maybe you'll go back and start from what feels like zero; however, each time you do that, you've learned a lot, and you bring all that with you, so the next time it goes faster. Still, sometimes it's hard to have resilience.

For some people it's easier for them to let go and move on to the next thing. For some it's more of a challenge. Either way, it's important to recognize when things aren't working and to reset; the faster the better! I've cycled back. And plenty of other successful entrepreneurs have too. It's a healthy sign of your growth and progress. Wouldn't it be great to be able to see what it is you need to move toward a business and life you love?

Let me tell you about working with Sandra. Sandra was a journalist, and she had an idea for how to help people use their stories to tell folks about their businesses and help with their marketing. As part of the Inspiration step, we pretty quickly identified a way to adapt that idea to suit a particular group we were involved with and a way to serve those folks.

She put that together, and we figured out a way for her to sponsor a particular event and make her offer to help people with that. I also worked closely with her to see what her process was like and to help her put some structure in place that would support her in working with that particular group. That's the kind of Inspiration and real-world Steps she got in the structure. Those are the third, fourth, and fifth parts of my system.

Sandra sent me a note. She wrote, "His gift is seeing possibilities others miss! And he encouraged me to create a structure so I can leverage this." It was so great seeing her take the leap and fly.

How to Get Clear about Your Next Move in Building Your Business

Let's talk about how to get clear about your next move in building your business around your passions and your life, rather than having your business taking over everything.

Let's take stock of where we are right now. The S.A.L.S.A. Scan™ solves the problem of getting clear about what you love to do and do well, and of finding your sweet spots. And we also talked about how to use it to start moving in the direction you want to go.

Once you've found your sweet spots, what's left to complete the picture?

We can even dig deeper with my system for finding a business idea that's right for you

First of all, like I mentioned in Sean's story: What's important in your life, what's non-negotiable? As I discussed in Barbara's story: What's your vision for what you want and a path to get you there? What are the real-world steps you can take right now? Let's put some structures in place that will support your success. I have a system with templates and structures to walk you through all of this step-by-step.

Sandra loved the story that I'm going to tell you next so much that she told me I have to tell it to others. Remember I mentioned I was a gymnast in high school? In the fall we would practice for competitions, and in the spring, after we finished the competitions, we would begin practicing for a circus.

During our school's spring break, we would throw all of our equipment in the back of a big bus and travel to various places in the southeast U.S., giving shows at schools, churches, campgrounds, and those sorts of places. It was quite something.

In addition to the usual gymnastics tumbling, we had clowns, juggling, tightrope walking, diving through flaming hoops, and all those sorts of things. I did an adagio routine with a girl named April where I'd lift her up in various poses. The big event of the show was a trapeze act. I was the catcher on the trapeze.

I remember when we were doing a show on the border between North and South Carolina the summer of my senior year. We'd had all of the equipment set up, but we didn't realize that between the time we set up the equipment and the time the show started, it had lightly misted.

During the first tumbling run, everybody was slipping and sliding all over the place, so we took a pause and wiped everything down and proceeded with the show. When it came time for the trapeze act, I was the catcher on the trapeze, so I got up there, wiped down my bar, put some stickum on my hands, and was all set to go.

A guy named Greg did the very first trick. Fortunately, he was a little smaller and a little lighter. Greg went to throw his first trick, which was a really simple move—just a simple release and catch, nothing fancy; however, they had forgotten to wipe down the bar that the fliers were using, and Greg slipped. He came flying by me. I reached out and grabbed a couple of fingers on one of his hands, and he looked up at me with eyes as big as saucers. I could see the terror in his eyes, and it was pretty scary for me too. I had him reach up and grab my other hand, and I swung him and dropped him down into the net. We wiped down the bar and proceeded with the show. I'm proud to say I never missed a catch in a show.

I want to make a couple of points about this anecdote. First of all, the trapeze is a great metaphor; if you're going to do any of the kinds of things that we were just talking about—if you want to fly—you have to let go. If you do and you're working with me, I'll be there to catch you.

The other thing I want to say is that you don't learn a trick by just going up there and throwing a flip with a twist and knocking it out of the park the first time around. You don't start by having it locked in. When you start out, we put you in a harness with somebody holding the rope. You practice a bit and give it a try until you're able to hit that trick successfully on a regular basis. Then we remove the harness, and off you go. It's the same with a business; sometimes it takes a while before you can get yourself flying consistently. If you fly, I'll be there to catch you. And when you're ready, I'll let you go. And you can always come back.

When I was traveling for business, I saw an ad that somebody posted. It was one of those sheets of paper with the ad across the top and those little tear-away strips on the bottom, but this ad really caught my eye; I took a picture of it. On the top it said, "Take at least one." The tear-off tabs said, "A chance."

Are you ready to take a chance? Are you ready to give something a try? My dad prudently didn't. He ended up backing off and not taking a chance with his business, but Sean and Sandra were both willing to make the leap, and it really worked out for them.

I've made my own leaps. I invested in myself and went back to school, I moved from the technical side of work to the business side, and now I'm in my own business.

A mistake many people make is to spend their time thinking and dreaming, rather than doing what it takes to quickly get clear, focused, and in action on a business idea that is right for them.

When I worked more closely with Brenda, we looked for ways she could expand her business. She said, "Eric has a very unique ability to see possibilities that others miss. Every time I work with him, I walk away with exciting ideas for my business that I had never even considered. And his ideas are a combination of simple things I could do very quickly and other things that support more of a long term vision of my business. If you are looking for ideas on how to expand your business or ways to run your business in a more profitable way, you need to talk to Eric. Or maybe you're just feeling stuck, bored, or tired with your business. Eric can help."

Gina had a successful online business which involved recurring licensing. As a baseline, we reviewed her current business model and methods, then identified some new ways for encouraging additional licensees. In her own words, "In the first hour of talking to Eric, it was as if the sunshine came out. He gave me clarity in an area that I had struggled with for over a year. This has opened up an entirely new way to expand my business and take it to the next level. Eric knew exactly what questions to ask, and how to help me get from point A to point B, when all I saw was fog. In addition, I got at least three good ideas that I can implement right away. So I'm really excited and I can't wait to see the results!"

Jen was seeking ways to leverage her successful copywriting business. To set a baseline, we worked more closely to assess her current approach and identify some key things to change. We laid out a path for building toward her goals and she has been continuing to expand her leveraged business. Here's what she had to say: "Thank you for pointing me in the right direction, Eric. In a very short time you showed me the clearest, easiest course of action to achieve fast results. I was relieved to find that the foundation was already in place, so I'm confident I'll be able to quickly implement the steps we talked about. What's more, you painted a picture of some truly viable options for taking my business to another level very soon. Your business acumen and creativity - not to mention keen listening skills - are so very much appreciated! Thanks for believing in me and holding me accountable."

I really have a passion for supporting busy, successful people like you, so I decided to create a unique opportunity for the people reading this. I'm offering you an opportunity to have a private, one-on-one B.L.I.S.S. Builder™ Discovery Session with me at no cost. This one-on-one session has a $500 value. Even if we never talk again after the session, you will get more clarity about your best next move in creating your business around your passions and your life.

There is one catch: You need to qualify. I have a limited number of slots, so the people who qualify will be contacted by email within three business days and given the opportunity to schedule their sessions. The sessions are scheduled on a first-come, first-serve basis, so it's in your best interest to reply and schedule right away. If I don't hear from you within three days, your session will be given to the next person on the waiting list.

Are you like me, and like seeing things laid out? Just check out GettingInspiredNow.com/go.

Let's walk through that online form and I'll tell you who these sessions are for.

The first item is, "Yes, I'm ready for a business and life I love. Schedule me for a free B.L.I.S.S. Builder™ Discovery Session."

Now let's go through the rest. On the online form, check all the boxes that apply in order to be considered. Here they are:

- Today's talk really spoke to me. I don't want to settle. I want a business and life I love.

- I am ready to have a frank conversation about getting back in touch with that passion, that inspiration, that excitedness and getting clarity on my next best move.

- I've been successful, but I feel like I sacrificed who I am at my core to make it work.

- I know my lack of clarity is holding me back, and I'm ready to change that.

- I know I need to do something, and I'm not sure what.

- I have an "invest in myself" mindset. When I see I need help, I invest the time, energy, or money to get the help I need.

- I highly value this offer, and I fully commit to showing up for my BLISS Builder™ Discovery session, ready to take action on suggestions I receive.

There's a place for your name (first and last name), your best email address, your best phone number, and then one last check box: "Yes, if I qualify, I will make every effort to schedule my one-on-one B.L.I.S.S. Builder™ Discovery Session within three days of being notified. I understand if I don't, I will forfeit my session." At the bottom there's a little box to click – "Tell me if I qualify" – and that sends off your information.

You may be worried that this is going to be a sales pitch. That is not my style. Of course, if you want to learn what it will be like to work with me, we can certainly discuss that on the call. However, my main objective is to have you walk away with more clarity about your best next move with creating a business around your passions and your life.

I like to make sure I have time to focus on each individual, so I'm only available for a limited number of openings. When you apply, I can only hold your spot for three days, so please fill out the form in full at GettingInspiredNow.com/go. If you qualify, I'll email you shortly, and you must schedule your session within three days or it will go to someone else on the waiting list.

Your work is important, and people need you. I want to make sure you get the support you need. I really look forward to talking with you.

Here's How to Get Clear about What You Love to Do and Do Well

Are you just not sure what you want to do, even though you've been successful and feel like you should know? Do you feel like you're spinning in circles, dispersing your energy in too many directions? Do you feel like you're compromising, doing what you do well and what people want, but it isn't the authentic you?

That's where we come in. We help people just like you get clear about what you love to do and do well, so you can focus your energy on a clear, purposeful goal that calls to your heart and start producing the results you want. Finally! A proven process for getting clarity about your best next move with creating a business around your passions and your life, rather than your business taking over everything.

Discover the proven methodology for getting results, which all starts with getting really clear about what you are passionate about. We'll share with you the structures to help you systematically get clear and put a plan in place so you can start getting the results you want.

Most people think they need to just dig down and work harder and longer to have more success in their lives. Now you can get clear about what you love to do and do well to start getting the results you really want.

To get started, simply visit: GettingInspiredNow.com/go today.